I0602078

NO LONGER
PROPERTY OF PPLD

PIKES PEAK LIBRARY DISTRICT

16700873 9

BEGINNING HISTORY

NORMAN CASTLES

Graham Rickard

Illustrated by Michael Bragg

The Bookwright Press
New York · 1990

PROPERTY OF
PIKES PEAK LIBRARY DISTRICT
P.O. BOX 1579
COLORADO SPRINGS, CO 80901

BEGINNING HISTORY

J
942.
R539n

Crusaders
Egyptian Pyramids
Greek Cities
Norman Castles

All words that appear in **bold** are explained in the glossary on page 22.

First published in the United States in 1990 by
The Bookwright Press, 387 Park Avenue South, New York, NY 10016

First published in 1989 by Wayland (Publishers) Limited
61 Western Road, Hove, East Sussex, BN3 1JD.

© Copyright 1989 Wayland (Publishers) Ltd

Library of Congress Cataloging-in- Publication Data
Rickard, Graham.
Norman castles/by Graham Rickard.
p. cm. – (Beginning history)
Bibliography: p.
Includes index.
Summary: A simple history of Norman castles describing their origins, how they were built,
the defense of the castles, and their daily life within the castle walls.
ISBN 0–531–18323–8
1. Castles – England – history – Juvenile literature. 2. Normans – England – History –
Juvenile literature. 3. Great Britain – History – Norman period, 1066–1154 Juvenile literature.
[1. Castles. 2. Normans – England – Social life and customs.]
I. Title.   II. Series: Beginning history (New York, N.Y.)
DA660.R53 1990   89–34447
942 – dc20   CIP
                                                                  AC

Typeset by Kalligraphics Limited, Horley, Surrey.
Printed in Italy by G. Canale & C.S.p.A.

CONTENTS

WHO WERE THE NORMANS?

The word Norman means man from the north. The first Norman people were Viking warriors from **Scandinavia**, who **invaded** an area of Northern France that is now called Normandy.

The Normans had a feudal system of government, which meant that peasants served their local lord, or **baron**, in return for strips of land on which they could grow food. In the same way, all the lords served their king in return for having control over their own area. The Normans were very good soldiers. Norman **knights** wore metal **armor** and rode horses when fighting their enemies.

A Norman lord surveys his lands as he returns to his castle from a hunting trip.

The barons built strong castles to defend themselves, and these castles soon became important centers of feudal society. The Norman castle was the baron's home and fortress. It was also bank, prison, police station, tax office, and law court for the area that he controlled.

A scene from the **Bayeux Tapestry** *of Norman knights galloping into battle.*

5

NORMAN INVADERS

After settling in northern France, the Normans began to invade other parts of Europe, and soon had control of Sicily and southern Italy.

In the year 1066, the Norman king, William the Conqueror, decided to invade England. He gathered his army on the French coast and sailed across the English Channel to claim the English throne. The English **Saxon** king, Harold, marched his army south to stop the Norman invaders, and the two armies met at

Above *A foot soldier in full armor, carrying his weapons and shield.*

Right *The Norman fleet crossing the English Channel on their way to invade England.*

6

the Battle of Hastings, not far from
the coast where the Normans had
landed. King Harold was killed in the
battle, and William was crowned as
the new English king.

As the Normans conquered the rest
of England, they built hundreds of
small wooden castles to protect
themselves, and from which they
could control the local people.

*The coronation of
King William I of
England, after he
defeated King
Harold at the Battle
of Hastings.*

WOODEN CASTLES

The first Norman castles were quickly built to protect the Norman barons and their knights, and to control the local Saxon people. Some early castles were circular banks of earth surrounded by a ditch. Others, called motte-and-bailey castles, had a square wooden fort, or **keep**, built on top of a mound of earth, called the **motte**. The keep was surrounded by a fence of sharp wooden stakes. It was the safest part of the castle. At the foot of the motte was a circular courtyard inside another wooden fence; this courtyard was called the

The Normans building their first castle at Hastings. On the left, two are fighting a mock battle.

8

bailey. The bailey contained kitchen, stables, bakery and chapel. Outside the fence was a deep ditch, sometimes filled with water, which could only be crossed over a **drawbridge**. The drawbridge was raised if the castle was attacked.

These wooden castles could be easily burned or smashed with **battering rams**, and many were soon replaced with stronger stone castles.

A Saxon tribe makes a surprise attack on a Norman castle, and sets fire to the wooden buildings.

STONE CASTLES

This strong stone castle at Rochester in Kent has walls 3.6 m (12 ft) thick.

The Normans built castles in large towns, along borders, and to protect important river crossings and roads. They replaced their wooden castles with stone ones, which were much stronger. The Tower of London is the most famous of the Normans' stone castles, but there are many others that still survive. These castles have thick outer walls, with towers and gaps at the top called **battlements**, from which **archers** fired their arrows. Inside the walls a strong stone keep was built.

On the ground floor of the keep was a storeroom for weapons and armor. Above was the main hall, where the lord and his lady entertained guests and ate their meals. They slept in the top room of the keep, called a **solar**. Most castles had a chapel. Some even had a toilet, which was called a **garderobe**. This was just a hole in the castle wall.

solar spiral staircase battlements

pel

inner
castle wall

t hall

nory

room

The stone keep of a Norman castle was built on three levels. The
thick outer walls had passages and stairways inside them.

BUILDING CASTLES

Building a castle was very hard work and required a large number of skilled people.

Building a stone castle was an enormous task. There was very little construction machinery, and the castle took thousands of men several years to complete. Castles were very expensive to build, and each one cost enormous sums of money.

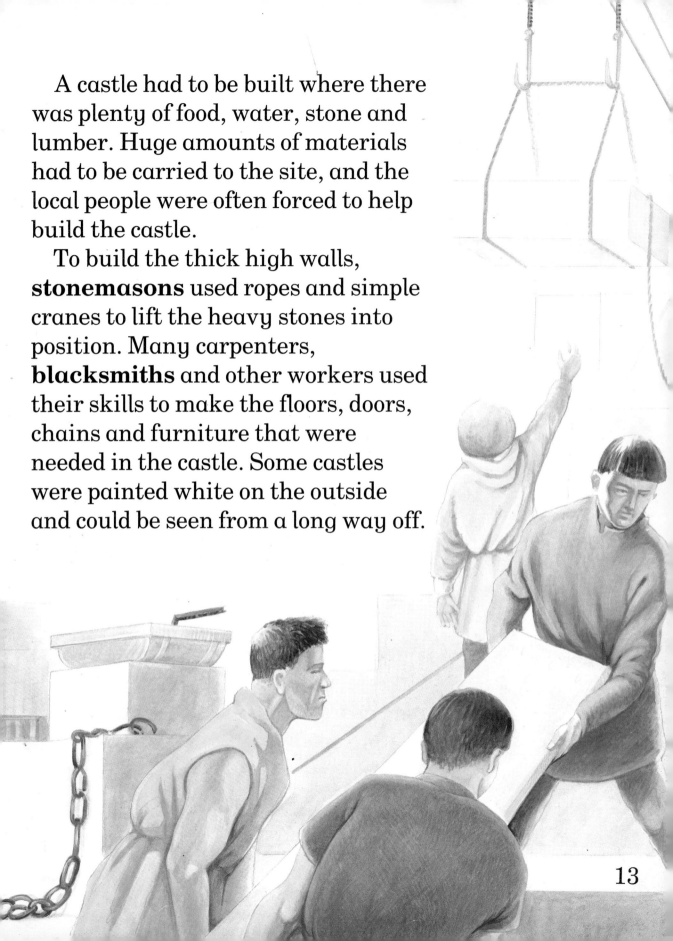

A castle had to be built where there was plenty of food, water, stone and lumber. Huge amounts of materials had to be carried to the site, and the local people were often forced to help build the castle.

To build the thick high walls, **stonemasons** used ropes and simple cranes to lift the heavy stones into position. Many carpenters, **blacksmiths** and other workers used their skills to make the floors, doors, chains and furniture that were needed in the castle. Some castles were painted white on the outside and could be seen from a long way off.

13

ATTACKING AND DEFENDING A CASTLE

Soldiers attack a castle using a huge catapult to hurl rocks over the walls. The defenders fire arrows and pour down boiling water.

Castles were very difficult to attack. Archers fired their arrows from the battlements, and the entrance to the castle was often guarded by a drawbridge and gatehouse. The gatehouse had a metal gate, called a **portcullis**, which was lowered in times of attack. Once inside the gatehouse, attackers faced a hail of arrows fired from slits in the side walls, and large stones, or boiling water dropped from the roof.

Attacking armies might use ladders to climb the castle walls, or try to smash the gates and walls with battering rams. Or they might tunnel beneath the walls and light a fire to make them collapse. They also used huge **catapults** to fire rocks and burning spears over the walls.

A long **siege** was the most common form of attack, and sometimes lasted many months. The attackers kept all supplies from entering the castle, and the people inside had to surrender or starve to death.

PEOPLE IN A CASTLE

A Norman castle was both a home and a fortress. Besides the lord and lady with their family and friends, fifty people or more lived inside the castle.

After the baron, the most important person in the castle was the **steward**, a knight who was left in charge of the castle when the baron was away. He organized the running of the castle and its lands, and looked after his lord's money.

Above *Coins from the reign of King William I.*

Below *The armorer checks the blade of a sword while a kitchenmaid pours beer, and a boy carries bread from the kitchen.*

16

Other officials looked after the castle's supplies of food, drink and firewood, and many servants were needed to wash and mend clothes, look after the horses, and carry supplies. Cooks, bakers and brewers produced great quantities of food and beer, while the **armorer** made sure that the soldiers had plenty of bows, arrows, swords and armor.

Carpenters and stonemasons kept the castle in good repair. The priest performed his religious duties and also taught the lord's children.

Two Normans sit down to a meal of wine and cheese. Colorful tapestries were hung on the walls to make the room warmer.

EVERYDAY LIFE

The castle bailey contained gardens and orchards. Pigs and chickens roamed freely.

Life in a castle was always busy. The lord inspected his lands, and his steward made sure that the farmers paid taxes and provided food for the castle. The lord was also the local judge, and decided what punishments should be given to people who had broken the law.

The cooks got up very early and worked in the bailey to provide food for all the people in the castle. Many people worked in the nearby forests, cutting firewood for the ovens and open fires in the castle.

Most castles had a well to provide water, but it was the **brewer's** job to make the beer that everyone drank with their meals. Gardeners grew vegetables and herbs and kept pigs, cattle, chickens and bees inside the castle walls.

In the stables, the grooms looked after the horses. The soldiers sharpened their weapons and practiced their archery. They took turns in keeping a watch for enemies who might attack.

In the **forge** the blacksmith made swords, spears and shields, and other weapons. He also made horseshoes and kitchen pots and pans.

A carved ivory ornament showing Normans playing chess.

CASTLE AMUSEMENTS

Living in a castle was not all hard work. There were plenty of things to keep people amused in their spare time. For the lord and his friends, the favorite sport was hunting. They rode on horses, using dogs and **falcons** as well as bows and arrows to hunt deer, wild boar and other animals, which they brought back to the castle to be cooked.

Most people lived, ate and slept together. In the evenings, they ate at large tables in the great hall, using knives and fingers, because there were no forks. Bones and scraps were thrown to the dogs on the floor, which was covered with straw.

After the meal, people played games such as chess, draughts (checkers) or dice. Sometimes there were jugglers, musicians or story-tellers.

Occasionally there were exciting contests called **tournaments**, in which knights in armor using blunt lances, tried to knock each other off their horses.

When the lord and his lady went upstairs to bed, everyone else wrapped themselves in blankets and lay on the floor to sleep.

Entertainments in the great hall.

GLOSSARY

Archers Men skilled in using bows and arrows as weapons.

Armor Metal protection for soldiers and horses.

Armorer A man who looked after weapons and armor.

Bailey The outer part of a castle.

Baron A Norman lord.

Battering ram A tree trunk used to knock holes in a castle wall.

Battlements The top parts of the castle walls, made with gaps like missing teeth through which the archers fired arrows.

Bayeux Tapestry An 11th century embroidery depicting the Norman invasion of England.

Blacksmith Someone who makes and mends articles of iron.

Brewer A maker of beer.

Catapult A heavy war engine used for hurling stones.

Drawbridge A bridge that can be raised and lowered.

Falcon A kind of bird used for hunting.

Forge A place where a blacksmith works, making things from metal.

Garderobe (pronounced "gard-robe") A simple toilet in a castle.

Invade To use military force to enter and occupy a country.

Keep The strong inner tower of a castle.

Knight A man who served his lord as a mounted soldier.

Motte A mound of earth with a keep on top.

Portcullis A large metal gate that was raised or lowered.

Saxons The people who lived in England before the Normans invaded.

Scandinavia Three countries of northern Europe: Sweden, Norway and Denmark.

Siege An attempt to capture a fortress or town by surrounding it so that those inside will be starved out.

Solar The top room of the keep, used as the lord's bedroom.

Steward Someone who manages an estate.

Stonemason Someone who prepares stone for building.

Tournament An event where mounted knights compete against each other with lances.

BOOKS TO READ

The Age of Chivalry by Sylvia Wright (Warwick, 1988)

The Black Death by James Day (Bookwright, 1989)

Castles and Crusaders by Philip Sauvain (Warwick, 1986)

Richard the Lionheart and the Crusades by Christopher Gibb (Bookwright, 1985)

Richard the Lionhearted by Joanne Jessop (Bookwright, 1989)

Medieval Castles by Brian Adams (Gloucester, 1989)

William the Conqueror and the Normans by Robin May (Bookwright, 1985)

INDEX

Picture Acknowledgments

The illustrations appearing on the following pages were provided by: Michael Holford 5, 6 (lower), 8, 10; Ronald Sheridan 16, 19; Wayland Picture 6 (top), 17. Artwork on page 11 is by Jenny Hughes.

PROPERTY OF
PIKES PEAK LIBRARY DISTRICT
579
COLORADO SPRINGS, CO 80901